By His Side

Presented to

Diane Sullivan
Sanders

By

The Maurice Baldwin

August 1972

By His Side
- A Woman's Place

by
LOIS McBRIDE TERRY

BROWNLOW PUBLISHING, INCORPORATED
P. O. BOX 3141
FORT WORTH, TEXAS 76105

BROWNLOW GIFT BOOKS

Contents

This book is dedicated to my husband;

By his side, I was inspired to begin it;

By his side, I was encouraged to continue it;

By his side, I was enabled to finish it;

By his side, I am committed to live it.

—MRS. CHEM TERRY

I

From This Day Forward

EVERY little girl loves to dream of her wedding day. The church will be a fairyland of blossoms and candles and smiling faces. The groom will be so handsome and the bride so beautiful that, when he lifts her white-cloud veil for that blissful kiss, an audible sigh will ascend from the lips of an appreciative audience. The ceremony may differ from girl to girl, but one single desire expresses itself in every girl's dream: she wants her wedding to be a beautiful one.

And that is as it should be. God intended that every little girl should be able to dream of a beautiful wedding, and a truly beautiful marriage. He placed that dream in orbit on the sixth day of creation, when the world was very new.

"And the Lord God said: it is not good that man should be alone, I will make an help meet for him. . . . And the rib which the Lord God had taken from man, made he a woman, and brought her unto the man. . . . Therefore shall a man leave his father and his mother, and shall cleave unto his wife: and they shall be one flesh" (Gen. 2:18,22, 24). This is the sacred story of the very first marriage. Jesus quoted God's law in Matthew 19:5, adding in verse 6, ". . . . What therefore God hath joined together, let not man put asunder."

Because it was first her Heavenly Father's dream, every little girl can continue to dream of the husband and home she will have one day. This is not a selfish aspiration; it is a high and holy ambition, if God's plan is understood and honored.

"It is not good for man to be alone . . . ." When God in His Wisdom made that profound declaration, he was paying every woman the highest compliment she could ever receive. *Because man needed her, God made woman.* She has been fashioned by the Foremost Designer to be an appropriate helper for her husband. *Hers is no minor role. It is permanent, significant, and, yes, glamorous.*

Permanent. "Love is strong as death . . . Many waters cannot quench love, neither can the floods drown it" (Song of Solomon 8: 6,7). Christ said, "Whosoever shall put away his wife, except it be for fornication, and shall marry another, committeth adultery: and whoso marrieth her which is put away doth commit adultery" (Matt. 19:9). The marriage vow is for life.

> Perhaps the greatest blessing in marriage is that it lasts so long. The years, like the varying interests of each year, combine to buttress and enrich each other. Out of many shared years, one life. In a series of temporary relationships, one misses the ripening, gathering, harvesting joys, the deep hard-won truths of marriage.
> — Richard C. Cabot

From *WHAT MEN LIVE BY*. By permission of Houghton Mifflin Company, publishers.

Significant. History teaches us that there is no substitute for righteous wives and mothers if we are to have righteous nations. It is not by accident that Sarah, Jochabed, Hannah, Elizabeth, and Eunice had courageous husbands and faithful sons. They were women of great courage and faith. Might not the record of Ahab, Lot, and Annanias have read differently, but for Jezebel, Lot's wife, and Sapphira?

> The ideal which the wife and mother makes for herself, the manner in which she understands duty and life, contain the fate of the community. Her faith becomes the star of the conjugal ship, and her love the animating principle that fashions the future of all belonging to her. Woman is the salvation or destruction of the family. She carries its destinies in the folds of her mantle.
>
> — Henri F. Amiel

Of all human relationships, there are none more enduring than those of family and home. Of all human endeavors, there is none more significant than that of a wife-mother-homemaker.

Glamorous. It is the most love-centered of all professions. Its pre-requisites are only the feminine qualities of warmth, generosity, and understanding. Only the truly lovely can qualify.

An appreciative husband wrote:

> Brightest truth, purest trust in the universe . . . .
> > all were for me
> > > In the kiss of one girl.
> > > > — Robert Browning

Another famous poet lyricized the glamour of marriage in these words:

> There's a bliss beyond all that the minstrel has told,
> When two, that are link'd in one heavenly tie,
> With heart never changing, and brow never cold,
> Love on through all ills, and love on till they die.

One hour of a passion so sacred is worth
Whole ages of heartless and wandering bliss;
And oh! if there be an Elysium on earth,
It is this — it is this!

—Thomas Moore

The dictionary defines glamour as "fascination, enchantment, charm." Of all careers for women, there is none more glamorous than the permanent and significant career of "an help meet" for man.

When both husband and wife recognize the Hand of God in the creation of wife for husband, the marriage relationship becomes beautiful indeed. Neither self-seeking nor self-sufficiency can survive in such a healthy environment. For the wife finds fulfillment in knowing she is needed — who does not *need* to be needed? The husband gains strength by acknowledging weakness. Because each one without the other is incomplete, both can say with the One who made them so, "It is not good for man to be alone." And every faithful wife will add her own prayer-size postscript, "Thank you, Dear Father, for placing me right where I want to be — by his side!"

From this day forward. On her wedding day, the bride takes her place beside the man she loves, to be his companion, his complement, his counterpart. The past becomes a shadowy backdrop of figures, facts, and faces — important only because they somehow helped to shape the present exciting moment. The future is all now. And it is for two:

. . . . I feel that I shall stand
Henceforward in thy shadow. Nevermore
Alone upon the threshold of my door
Of individual life, I shall command
The uses of my soul, nor lift my hand

Serenely in the sunshine as before,
Without the sense of that which I forbore —
Thy touch upon the palm. The widest land
Doom takes to part us, leaves thy heart in mine
With pulses that beat double. What I do
And what I dream include thee, as the wine
Must taste of its own grapes. And when I sue
God for myself, He hears that name of thine,
And sees within my eyes the tears of two.

— Elizabeth Barrett Browning

II

Forsaking All Others

COUNTLESS women have stood before ministers and magistrates, promising "I will forsake all others for the one by my side." This is one of the most sacred promises a woman will ever make — second only to the vow she makes to God on becoming a Christian. It is a moment to remember, and to cherish. Only one moment, yet its length cannot be measured in seconds, nor even in days. For if the moment has meaning, it will last a lifetime. And it should have had its beginning long before the words were uttered. No sudden whim — no spur-of-the-moment decision will do. "Believing that God has ordained marriage, and has decreed that it shall join one man and one woman for life, I will take this man unto my wedded husband . . . . forsaking all others."

What does it mean, this rather heartless-sounding phrase, *"forsaking* all others?" Must one really *forsake* others? A misunderstanding or misapplication of the words will result in much needless unhappiness. *There are many who must not be forsaken.*

"Forsaking all others" *does not include God,* else a Christian could not promise it. No matter how much she may *love her husband,* a wife continues to *worship only God,* and to hear Christ say, "He that loveth father or mother . . . son or daughter . . . more than me is not worthy of me"

(Matt. 10:37). Loving one's husband cannot cancel the first commandment: "Thou shalt love the Lord, thy God . . ." (Matt. 12:30).

It does not include the assembly, for that would be both disobedient to God and inconsiderate of others. "And let us consider one another . . . Not forsaking the assembling of ourselves together . . ." (Heb. 10:24,25). A wife who truly loves her husband will never use him as an excuse for missing worship services.

It does not include parents, whom she is to honor ". . . that it may be well with thee, and that thou mayest live long on the earth . . ." (Eph. 6:2,3). When God said that a man should *leave* father and mother, he did not mean that parents should be *left out* of their married children's lives. Parents are not to be left lonely, uncared for, forsaken. Love for husband will neither inspire nor explain such cruelty.

It does not include the needy, for she must practice pure religion which demands an active interest in all who have afflictions (James 1:27). She knows, also, that God has promised either a *curse* or a *blessing* on her home, depending upon her own attitude toward the poor. "He that giveth unto the poor shall not lack: but he that hideth his eyes shall have many a curse" (Prov. 28:27). The valuable wife, described in Proverbs 31, ". . . stretcheth out her hand to the needy; yea, she reacheth forth her hands to the poor." Jesus taught that the poor are as permanent as marriage (Matt. 26:11). Remembering the needs of her husband does not justify forgetting the needs of others.

It does not include friends, for true friendship, also, is permanent. "A friend loveth at all times . . ." (Prov. 17:17). Love for friends is one of the proofs of Christian discipleship, for Jesus said, "By this shall all men know ye are my disciples if ye have love one to another" (Jno. 13:35). He demonstrated the depth of His friendship: "Greater love hath no man than this, that a man lay down his life for his friends" (Jno. 15:13). Loyalty to one's new husband cannot command a corresponding disloyalty to one's old friends. Nor will it forbid the cultivation of new friendships, for God said first what all have learned by experience and observation, "A man that hath friends must show himself friendly . . ." (Prov. 18:24). Some of the *unhappiest* couples on earth are those that have tried to build fences around their love, forbidding friends to disturb their *happiness.* A wife who would enter into marriage, planning to shut her doors to friends would be better off to stay single.

Since the taking of a husband does not take the place of all previous commitments, it follows that the ideal marriage is one in which both partners recognize their dependence upon God, their need to aid the needy, and their right to welcome friends. It adds immeasurably to the joys of home-making to realize that both husband and wife are building with God, and that His laws are on their side, to help them as they make their lives and their home a source of blessing to all the lives and homes they touch. When both partners love each other, honor their parents, help the poor, welcome friends, and reverence God, they cannot fail to find the highest possible good. Since this is true, wealthy indeed is the wife who can say to her husband:

I married rich.
Fortunate me!
You wear your wealth
Becomingly:

Wisdom first;
You own a share.
Courage, too;
And strength to spare.

You're holding a
Monopoly
On rare old
Generosity;

Kindness;
Understanding; Love.
Your Wisdom
"Cometh from above."

You have the market
Cornered fast
On all good things;
But, best and last:

Rich toward God.
Your greatest worth?
A Reverent Heart.
I own the earth!

— L. T.

If "forsaking all others" does not include God, the assembly, parents, the needy, and friends, what does it include? *Who is to be forsaken?* There are two groups, and one of those will seem a contradiction.

Family and friends, when their interests would conflict with one's responsibility as a wife. God did say, ". . . leave . . . father and mother . . ." He did declare, ". . . let wives be (subject) to their own husbands in everything" (Eph.

5:24). He does intend that a wife's first thought should be of her husband.

Nowhere in His Word can one find a young bride's "going home to Mother" after a lovers' quarrel. Nor is there any example of "running to Daddy" for a new coat, or the down-payment on a new home. *By his side* meant then what it still means: settling our own differences, and balancing our own budgets. Leaving father and mother out of both endeavors.

The wives who are approved in the Bible are "keepers *at* home" and "keepers *of* home." Can anyone imagine Sarah's leaving her "lord" to batch on leftovers, while she flitted here and there with the girls? And, among all the activities of the Virtuous Woman's busy day, ". . . she sitteth around her table all day with her friends," is not listed. If the good wives back then enjoyed their earlier equivalents of the modern coffee-breaks, surely they were not the constant and time-consuming affairs they have since become! And how, in the name of friendship, could Priscilla have gone bowling or played bridge when Aquila needed her so desperately to help him make tents, and teach Apollos? "Forsaking all others" means refusing to cultivate friends to the neglect of husband and home.

It includes all romantic ties. This would seem to go without saying, but it is not always as easy as it seems. Recently, a young girl's parents faced the wearisome task of recalling hundreds of wedding invitations, cancelling numerous orders from florists, caterers, photographers, and outfitters, and returning a small fortune in gifts to the givers. Their popular young daughter had decided, following the rehearsal dinner, that she could not bear the thought of giving up all her other admirers for the "one she loved."

A sadder example, by far, is the woman who discovered only *after* marriage that she was attractive to the opposite sex. The discovery was too much. She found herself, in turn, strongly attracted to other men — and guilty before God of unfaithfulness to her marriage vow. "Forsaking all others" forbids all future entanglements, as well as former romances.

Ideally, the decision is made well ahead of the promise. Indeed, if the forsaking has not already occurred, it is doubtful that *saying* can make it so. The words themselves may seem superfluous to one who is really prepared to say them.

> "Forsaking all others . . ." How can I say
> The words that would make me yours from this day?
> "Forsaking all others . . ." Why, Dear, don't you know
> All others *forsook me* — a long time ago.
> They vanished as surely as love for you came,
> The first time you smiled at me, called me by name.
> "Forsaking all others . . ." I never can do;
> There aren't any others — my whole world is you!
>
> — L. T.

III

His Good Right Arm

*Those who love us multiply our joys
and divide our sorrows.*

— H. O. Wilson

IN the marriage ceremony, ministers customarily remind the bride and groom that marriage is a holy estate instituted by God, approved by His Son, and regulated by the teachings of the apostles. In marriage, God has given man a *help meet;* the idea of "meet" implies likeness, correspondence in nature. "One like himself, as taken from him, the woman would be an aid and companion to the man in his tasks" (James Orr). One grateful husband said it this way: "She's my good right arm!"

Wherever Christianity's teachings and spirit prevail, woman is the loved companion, confidante, co-worker, and adviser to her husband. There will be a mutual sharing of all things: work and rest; trials and triumphs; burdens and blessings. A happy, successful wife lovingly demonstrates the lovely *helpfulness* of love. With Elizabeth Barrett Browning, she asks: " 'How do I love thee?' *Let me count some of the ways:*

"By helping you keep fit. You can eat with confidence the meals I shall set before you. For I will not stuff you with starches, starve you with fads, nor poison you with ignorance. Because your strength is in my keeping, I will

consider the planning and preparation of attractive nutritious meals to be my sacred responsibility — one of the ways I love you.

"Whether you are a 'day person' demanding eight hours' sleep every night, or one of the 'night people' who start to yawn about dawn, I promise to adjust — and co-operate. We shall, if you wish, decline all invitations except for sunrise breakfasts, and have friends in several *midnights* each month. I shall learn that television, like children, should be seen and not heard, and a rug is no less clean if it be vacuumed by moonlight. I shall spare no effort to insure your proper rest. This is one of the ways I love you — I put you to sleep!

"Although it may not be easy, I shall encourage you to exercise. Actually, there are many wholesome, invigorating activities we can share: a hike in the woods, a walk in the park, a set of tennis, a round of golf. Then, there is . . . mowing . . . and weeding . . . and . . . you'll get *plenty* of *exercise*, if I have my way!"

Just as proper food, rest, and exercise are necessary for his physical fitness, so the atmosphere of the home can affect the husband's mental health. One of the most important ways a wife can demonstrate her love for her husband is by helping him to keep his perspective, his sense of values, his sense of humor. Doubtless many mental breakdowns, even some suicides, have resulted from failure to give loved ones this assistance. A wife who can smile easily, laugh often, and even say occasionally, "So what?" will be able to keep her husband from taking himself too seriously, judging himself too harshly, hugging his hurts too closely. While it may or may not be true that back of every successful man there is a good woman, it is likely a fact that behind many miserable, ulcerated, nervous-wreck males there is a grumbling, grasping, neurotic female. Probably *most* cheerful, confident, and mentally-competent men do not go home to brooding, belittling wives.

"So, how do I love thee? With smiles, kisses, soothing words. With sometimes constructive criticism — more often, praise. Or, if you should choose, I shall but love thee better with *willing ears.*

"By helping you work well." Happy is the man whose wife understands the importance of his work. It is not a necessary evil to provide the material necessities of life: it is an expression of his personality, and more important, it is a part of his service to God. Whether he is an employer or an employee, the rule is the same:

> And whatsoever ye do, do it heartily as to the Lord and not unto men;
> Knowing that of the Lord ye shall receive the reward of the inheritance: for ye serve the Lord Christ.
>
> — Colossians 3:23,24

The passage above, as well as others (Col. 4:1; I Pet. 2:18; Eph. 6:5-9; I Tim. 6:1,2; Titus 2:9,10), emphasizes the motives for conscientious labor. Both employer and employee are Christ's servants who must account to Him; both do their work as service to Christ, to God's glory; both will receive reward or retribution from Christ.

Unfortunately, not all wives have the proper attitude toward work. Some are like *Mrs. Y* who lives on your block. Her husband is about to lose his job, mostly because of his well-meaning wife. *Mr. Y* has an important position with great responsibilities, and a generous salary. Instead of encouraging her husband to work "with good will," *Mrs. Y* has carried on a running battle with his company. "What do they think you are — a machine?" "They don't own you — or do they?" She has pitied him and petted him until he has become extremely temperamental and beligerant on the job, resenting his work, refusing responsibility, while accepting his paycheck as usual. Sooner or later, he will have to be replaced.

"How do I love thee? Here is one more way: by my attitude toward your work. It does not matter what your position might be — over a staff of hundreds or under one man. Whatever your salary, your status, your profits or losses, if every day you do your work honestly, heartily, with good will, to God's glory — you, my dear, are a *"Successful Man!"*

Helping a husband to work well may also require some lady-like elbow grease. One of the most attractive women in history, although nobody knows what she looked like, is Priscilla — faithful wife of Aquila. This woman, in the 18th chapter of Acts, wins admiration because of the way she helped her husband. Tent-making was hard work. Priscilla did not consider herself too good to do strenuous labor alongside her hard-working husband. With good will, and great skill, she did a man's work while keeping her woman's place.

"How do I love thee? By helping you work well. A breadwinner's responsibilities are great; your burdens are often heavy. I shall find my highest happiness in helping you to bear them.

ON GALATIANS 6:2,5
Your burden is yours while you're able to bear it;
When it becomes heavy, God tells me to share it.
God's love gave the order, so sweet, I'm confessing:
I can't tell the *burden*, sometimes, from the *blessing!*
— L. T.

"By helping you spend wisely, save regularly. What a way to love you!" These two unromantic characters go steady, and dull as they may seem, they should be carefully cultivated and warmly welcomed. For their absence can wreck a marriage, and destroy a home. Many of the marital troubles of our day are due to financial difficulties. A family which lives within its income, saving some small part at least, makes a much greater success of family life. Both wife and husband can make this side of their life a real expression of mutual regard and of team-work.

Whatever the circumstances, there will be need for planning and efficiency, in order to make the best use of money earned. That need calls for a budget. Any wife knows what a budget is: a foolproof plan to help us buy wisely, keep out of debt, and save something for *showers*. She knows, also, that they don't always work.

Like other best-laid plans of women and men, budgets often fail. *There are three popular pre-requisites to budget-failure:*

Failure to "consider one another . . ." (Heb. 10:24). As long as husband and wife continue to put themselves in competition for the income, each one striving to outspend the other, there will never be enough money to go around — budget or no budget!

Failure to develop the courage to live simply. One of the surest roads to budget-failure is the wasted effort to make a really big impression on *someone* with some *thing*. It can't be done. Most people who would be *impressed* are too busy trying to impress others! One of the greatest freedoms is the emancipation from the Joneses and their possessions. The glorious freedom to live happily on whatever scale *we* can comfortably afford!

Failure to keep a Christian attitude toward money and things. Poverty is not the greatest handicap, nor riches necessarily the greatest blessing. To sacrifice ease of mind to a misguided struggle for wealth, so that there is little room in life for love and fellowship, is to sacrifice the greater values for far lesser ones. Although the budget may look big, it may be a *big failure*.

"How do I love thee? By helping you spend wisely and save regularly. In my wifely concern for 'housing, furniture and equipment, food, clothing, running expenses, health, improvements, savings, and miscellaneous,' may I not forget that the true standard of living is an inner matter. Not how much the house cost, but what kind of people live within it? Not how fashionable the carpet is, but is there a welcome mat for friends? Not how handsome the table looks, but can we surround it with love and gratitude?

"And may I help you, also, to *be sure that God is given first place in our budget.* The generosity of your contribution may well depend on me, and my willingness to sacrifice.

"*By helping you play constructively.*" Good times together help to build a marriage. Strange that some women should find this way of loving hardest of all. A wife who has gladly learned to scrimp and save and sweat and slave for her husband will sometimes refuse to join him in a few hours of pleasant recreation. What a shame! For recreation recreates. It lightens burdens of fatigue and care. Every couple ought to plan plenty of these good times together.

One husband said, "Why, I'd rather have my wife along on a fishing trip than any man I know. She's my good buddy!" He might have added, "When I met her, she didn't know a fly-rod from a buggy-whip!" His wife might — just might — have some excellent advice for certain "golf widows."

Jesus placed his stamp of approval upon recreation of the right kind, at the right time, in the right amount. "Come ye apart . . . and rest awhile . . ." He invited His disciples (Mark 6:31). "Getting away from it all," occasionally, can help people who work hard to work better. There will be many burdens and cares that must be shared within the home, and without. Sharing the good times keeps the bad ones from becoming too big.

"I love thee, then, in this way too: I learn how to play your games. To share and enrich your leisure moments. To make your life *and mine* as full and as glowing as I possibly can. After all — anyone who can manage to balance a budget can certainly learn how to strike a tent. I *think* —

"By helping you grow spiritually." A husband has this obligation, even without his wife's help, for God has commanded it. But in no other way is her help more needed, and more noted. Every act of worship, every deed of service which he performs can be either helped or hindered by the woman he married.

Since the greatest of all arts is the art of living together, and since the highest and most permanent happiness depends upon it, and since the way to practice this art successfully lies through character, the all important question is how to obtain character. The surest way is through religion in the home.

— William Lyon Phelps

From *MARRIAGE.* By permission of
E. P. Dutton & Company, Inc., publishers

This is the wife's greatest contribution to her husband and to their children: to provide and encourage a spiritual atmosphere in the home. Faith in God should be not a mere formality which we go through occasionally, but an active, disciplining, driving force, influencing all the areas of our lives. Such a Christ-centered home gives purpose and dimension to the family and to the life of each member. It is next to impossible, however, without the inspiration and encouragement of a spiritually-minded wife and mother.

"How, then, must I love thee? By loving God more. By helping you to love Him, too. Because what I am can so easily determine what you — and our children — are likely to become, I shall not cease to pray daily:

Teach me, O Lord, the way of thy statutes;
and I shall keep it unto the end.
Give me understanding, and I shall keep thy law;
yea, I shall observe it with my whole heart.
Make me to go in the path of thy commandments:
for therein do I delight.
Incline my heart to thy testimonies, and not to
covetousness.
Turn away mine eyes from beholding vanity;
and quicken thou me in thy way.

— Psalms 119:33-37

IV

His Other Self

Wives, submit yourselves unto your husbands,
as unto the Lord.

— Ephesians 5:22

IN spite of the softened language of some popular marriage services, the word "obey" cannot be replaced with "cherish." Not as long as God commands, ". . . . wives be in subjection to your husbands . . ." and illustrates that subjection by saying, ". . . even as Sara obeyed Abraham . . ." (Eph. 5:22; I Pet. 3:1,6). *The submission which is every wife's responsibility is a part of her service to God,* and therefore, not at all affected by updated semantics. Marriages are made in Heaven — even in 1967!

Why should anyone find the word "submit" objectionable? It does not have to be. It simply means "to yield." In a negative sense, to submit is to "stop fighting against." True submission carries with it the idea of a "meek and quiet spirit" — a sweet peacefulness. Especially when the submission is to that one cherished above all others, "your own husband . . ." That one whom God tells to *love his wife as his own body* (Eph. 5:28). To submit to him is to give in to one's own self. In a sense, the wife *is* her husband; if not his *"better* half," at least his *"other* half" — *his other self.*

These thoughts take the sting out of the old-fashioned

version of the marriage ceremony. While they cannot change the word *obey* to *cherish*, they can help both wives and husbands to understand that one is a natural outgrowth of the other. Submission, obedience — these come easily when one loves and is loved. The difficult thing, it seems, would be to do otherwise. Who would want to fight against such unselfish love?

> To renounce your individuality, to see with another's eyes, to hear with another's ears, to be two and yet but one, to so melt and mingle that you no longer know you are you or another, to constantly absorb and constantly radiate, to reduce earth, sea and sky and all that in them is to a single being, to give yourself to that being so wholly that nothing whatever is withheld, to be prepared at any moment for sacrifice, to double your personality in bestowing it — that is love.
>
> — Gautier

Consideration is the key word, though unspoken, throughout the instructions to husbands and wives in the New Testament. The wife considers her husband, her head, and lovingly submits to his wishes. He, in turn, considers her, his own flesh, and "nourisheth and cherisheth her." It is not only her duty, then, but her pleasure, also, to keep herself so lovely and so loving that he would be willing to die for her, if necessary. This is what Paul is teaching in the fifth chapter of Ephesians.

He is teaching something else, also. There is a most practical lesson for wives included here in the very heart of a sublime analogy. *A wife is compared to the church.*

How is she like the church? "For the husband is head of the wife, even as Christ is head of the church: and he is saviour of the body" (v. 23).

What does this mean? "Therefore as the church is subject to Christ, so let the wives be to their own husbands in everything" (v. 24).

How does a wife demonstrate her subjection to her husband? The answer is found by extending the analogy. How does the church show its subjection to Christ? By recognizing His leadership, His authority.

By wearing His Name. Since ". . . there is none other name under heaven given among men, whereby we must be saved" (Acts 4:12), those who belong to Christ rejoice to wear His name. They love the sound of their name — *His Name.*

How like a new bride! The new name — her husband's — is music to her ears. She cannot hear it often enough! She loves the sight of it, too, and writes it, happily, at every opportunity. "Mrs. Johnson Benjamin Smith" — "Mrs. J. Benjamin Smith" . . . Mrs. Johnson B. Smith" . . . "Mrs. John Smith" . . . A wife honors her husband by wearing his name. *It means she belongs to him.*

Sometimes there are professional considerations which make it necessary for a married woman to keep her maiden name. While this may seem a good arrangement for business reasons, it does seem to take something away from the "oneness" of marriage. And, while it is not considered "etiquette," it is not uncommon to see a widow who continues to wear her deceased husband's full name till the day she dies. "Mrs. Jane Smith" may be proper; still, she prefers to be addressed as "Mrs. John B. Smith." *She loves his name.*

How else does a wife show herself to be subject to her

husband? *By obeying him.* Continuing the analogy, as the church is obedient to its Head, Christ, so she obeys her husband. She calls him "lord." When she understands the relationship, she will treasure her place. As "Christ . . . loved the church and gave himself for it" (v. 25), so her husband chose her, out of all the women in the world, to be his bride — to love her and to give himself for her! Would she knowingly disobey him? Not if she loves him.

She rejoices in his wisdom. She leans on his strength. When he asks for her opinion, she offers it; when he does not, she keeps silent. She even finds it in her heart to be grateful that she does not have to *make* the decisions, only *abide by them* as faithfully as she can. And if sometimes he should falter or fall, she encourages him. After all, he isn't really infallible, he is only a man. So she prays for him.

An unknown author advises a husband and wife to take care of each troubled moment in this positive way:

> Let moments of alienation if they occur, be healed at once. Never, no never, speak of it outside; but to each other confess and all will come out right. Never let the morrow's sun still find you at variance. Renew and renew your vow. It will do you good; and thereby your minds will grow together contented in that love which is stronger than death, and you will be truly one.

If she loves him, she will love to obey him. As the church loves to obey Christ. By her faithful, loving obedience, a wife demonstrates her subjection to her husband.

Perhaps the most revealing and rewarding discovery for wives and husbands is to notice that the words ". . . and they two shall be one flesh" are included in this passage,

Ephesians 5. The same passage which compares Christ and the church to husband and wife. The same passage which teaches wives to submit, to be in subjection to, and to reverence their husbands. The same passage which instructs husbands to love their wives as Christ loved the church, as their own bodies, as themselves. Surely if such unselfish love and such ungrudging submission were the spontaneous or automatic result of "getting married," there would be no need for such careful instructions in God's Word. It would seem, then, that *such oneness as God intends must be the result of constant care and attention.* It is an evidence of growth.

> It is a wise man who said that it is important not only to pick the right mate but to *be* the right mate. And contrary to so many popular love stories, it is not during the first year of bliss that most dangers crop up. Marriages do not, like dropped chinaware, smash as a result of that first quarrel which the newly married hope is unthinkable. Marriage is a rooted thing, a growing and flowering thing that must be tended faithfully.
>
> Lacking that mutual effort, we are apt to find some day that our marriage, so hopefully planted, has been withering imperceptibly. Gradually we realize that for some time the petals have lost their luster, and that the perfume is gone. Daily watering with the little gracious affectionate acts we all welcome, with mutual concern for the other's contentment, with self-watchfulness here and self-forgetfulness there, brings forth ever new blossoms.
>
> — Donald Culross Peattie
>
> Excerpt used with permission from "The Basic Axiom of Marital Felicity," by Donald Culroll Peattie. *The Reader's Digest*, October, 1941.

When God said, "For this cause shall a man leave his father and mother and shall be joined unto his wife, and they two shall be one flesh," He intended that a wife and her husband should grow together in such complete unity that they could be considered as *one*. In loving her, then, the husband would be loving himself. "He that loveth his wife loveth himself" (v. 28). To put asunder those whom God has so joined would be as brutal as tearing one's head from one's body, as agonizing as ripping one's flesh apart. It would be as difficult as dividing one from one's self!

Whenever a married couple has managed to achieve that perfect oneness with which God blesses those who follow his instructions, nothing on earth can greatly disturb their inner calm. A loving, submissive "other self" might express her quiet confidence and her love in these words:

> Then let quiet clap the mouth of morning,
> And slumber box the ears of Spring.
> While shadows gang to black the eye of beauty,
> Let singing's throat be slashed by sorrow's wing.
> And let the muscled back of youth be broken
> Embracing dying day — nor mind it much.
> For in the battered silence of old night,
> Our fingers touch.
>
> — L. T.

V

Meet "Mrs. Yes-Yes"

Let the wife see that she fear her husband.
— Ephesians 5:33 (R. V.)

A VERY young wife once wrote to her mother, "How can I *fear* my husband, when he is so sweet, and gentle — and loving? Tell me, Mother, you've never been afraid of Daddy; did you ever wonder about Eph. 5:33? Anyway — it seems to contradict another passage '. . . perfect love casteth out fear.'" In the last paragraph of her letter, the daughter wrote, "We'll see you next week-end, if Dick thinks best. What he says goes, you know!"

"Yes, I do know!" the mother replied. "And I know something else, too: you have answered your own question. Don't you see, Dear, it is your 'reverential fear' which causes you to write, 'What Dick says goes.' It is not the same 'fear' (dread, terror) of which John wrote. Love casts out such trembling uncertainty, while it inspires a calming trust, respect, and, yes, *reverence*. This is the confidence that you feel in Dick, and that I have always had in your father. No, I have never been afraid of Daddy, but I have *feared* him. What he says goes, too, you know!"

Every wife can be thankful that, in God's Word, the one person she is told to "reverence" is the one who has just been told to love her "even as himself." It ought to be so easy to become "Mrs. Yes-Yes" to someone who always considers her welfare *before* he makes any requests or issues any commands. The *harder* part, it would seem, would be *to say no* to such a one.

And yet, the language of the Lord suggests that there is a need for self-discipline in this respect. "Let . . . the wife *see* that she *reverence* her husband" (A.V.). She must not allow herself to slip into the habits and attitudes of disrespect and disobedience for husbands that have become so *fashionable* in today's society. She certainly must take care, must give it her deliberate attention, if she is to develop the reverential fear which God has commanded.

Seeing that she reverences her husband involves practice. It begins with her thoughts:

"I have never been able to stay angry with Tim," a wife complained. "I always end up by thinking about how *good* he is to me and the children, and how good it is to be his wife!"

Most wives would do well to spend some time every day considering "'how good it is!'" Every wife should, from time to time, deliberately contemplate the emptiness that would be her life without her husband. She can calmly calculate his worth by carefully enumerating his good qualities. How much more blessed is the moment spent in telling one's self a husband's virtues, than that spent in telling a neighbor his faults!

An unknown author expresses the silent intensity of a wife's devotion:

> Loving you so that when we walk in crowded places,
> Sudden my eyes grow misted with the veil of tears,
> So that I only see a blur where there were faces;

Loving you so that when my head is on your breast,
Words do not come and sudden thoughts go all unspoken;
Loving you so that just your reaching hands brings rest —
How can I ever let you know the love I bear you,
How can I tell you, dear, that true love never dies?
When words are only words and hands are only fingers,
When lips are only lips, and eyes are only eyes?

To quietly contemplate a husband's dearness and the great blessing it is just to love and be loved is to "see that she reverence her husband" in her thoughts.

To practice that wifely respect before others is the next step. It begins — and ends — in the home. Leading psychologists agree that the wife who usurps authority in the home weakens the unity of that home and threatens the very character of her own children. A child simply cannot respect a father who cannot, or will not, rule his own household. The wife who reverences her husband will desire that their children should respect him. She will never be guilty of these all-too-common practices:

Deceitfulness — "Don't tell your father. It's *our* little secret!"

Premature decisions — "It's all right with me. Ask your father."

Inconsistency — "You know what your daddy said, 'Absolutely not!' But — maybe just this once — go ahead. You have *my* permission."

Contradiction — "I don't care what your father said. He was wrong. You will do as *I* say!"

Disobedience — "Oh, look at that sporty convertible! Your father will be furious, but — I'll take it!"

Belittling — "Oh yes, your daddy's smart all right! And spineless! *All brains and no backbone!*"

On the positive side, a wife who wants her children to learn from her to respect their father will patiently and prominently portray, in all of her actions, these not-so-common attitudes:

"He is head of our house. Without him, our family would be unable to function smoothly, effectively, and happily. He does so much for all of us! We will honor him here.

"He is head of our house. As his family, we *care* what he thinks. We ask his opinions, and we pay attention to his suggestions. We love to please him in the little things: buying the brands he prefers, wearing the colors he likes us to wear, arranging the furniture the way he enjoys it. We respect his wishes — his unspoken wishes — as we respect his words.

"He is head of our house. With him, we can relax, and rely on his judgment and wisdom. Because we love him, we can tell the world — and say it with joy — 'What he says goes!' "

If every home in every land could be fashioned according to Christ's formula, on such mutual love and respect, how beautiful this world would be! With husbands loving their wives as themselves; with wives *seeing* that they reverence their husbands; with children learning unselfish love and respect from their parents, and passing those qualities on to the next generation — there would be little business for divorce courts and correctional institutions. While such a "Utopia" may seem a long way away — may never become a reality — let us never forget that it is embodied in

God's gracious commands. And every wife who has learned early to "fear her husband" has come to understand and appreciate the love of God in requiring it. Her home can become one small Utopia in a world that *wishes for* but *will not wait to find* the formula. Truly, her "cup runneth over!"

VI

Exhibit A-Plus

A TEENAGER watched an over-exposed television commercial showing a middle-aged husband, once again happy to be seen with his young-looking wife who had "hated that gray and washed it away."

"Oboy!" exclaimed the young girl. "She's got a problem, all right — but it's not on her head!"

Of course, husbands in general are not the shallow, vain, ridiculous individuals which the ad-makers would have us believe. Even the modern American husband, no doubt, still cares more deeply for his wife and his family than he does for his "image" or his "status symbols" — whatever those terms are supposed to mean. And a truly *impartial* survey would surely reveal that millions of women keep their hair gray because their husbands love them that way! Still, it is quite true that the right woman is a definite asset to a man. She is an integral part of his *image*, the Number One *symbol of his status* in the world of successful men. It is important for every man to choose the right woman to be his wife.

The right woman — what is she like? Who is this woman who is a credit to her husband? In some respects, each man would have his own individual answer to that question:

"Someone who thinks exactly like I do!"

"Someone who is my exact opposite!"

"Someone who likes a lot of activity!"

"Someone who'd rather relax and take it easy!"

"Someone who has a lot of ambition!"

"Someone who won't try to push me!"

Tastes may vary, and needs may differ, but there will be certain identical behavior characteristics common to all women who serve well the men whom they marry. According to the One Absolutely Reliable Authority, all the *right* women will:

> Love their husbands;
> Love their children;
> Think soberly;
> Keep chaste;
> Work at home;
> Show kindness;
> Obey their own husbands;
> ... that the word of God be not blasphemed. — Titus 2:4,5

When a wife serves her Lord by serving her husband in all these ways, her admirable behavior will be noticed. So plainly apparent, in fact, that it will keep even the most biased observer from saying one word against the Word of God. Surely if her consistent good-wife behavior can have that effect, it cannot but be a source of glory and honor to the man she has married.

The reverse is equally apparent: a man who might have been a "big wheel" in the eyes of men, has often been reduced to a pitiable, or laughable, "little spoke" by the persistent unbecoming conduct of his wife. Without half trying, most adults could name numerous examples of such status-shrinkers at work:

"Love their husbands?" There is Mr. A, a bank executive, whose wife flings her evil, unfounded, suspicions and jealous hatred on the ears of other executives' wives, employees, and bank customers. Most do not believe her; many think him weak for not putting a stop to her ravings; and some wonder ——.

"Love their children?" There is Mr. B, whose children are *hungry* for a mother's love. With her job, her club, her hobbies, and her *self* to occupy her time and exhaust her energy, Mrs. B has little left for the children she didn't especially want and the husband who is "able to manage so beautifully" without her. To the children, Mr. B is "Poor Pop!" To the neighbors, business associates, and social acquaintances, he has become "Nancy B's Baby Sitter." They shake their heads as they say it.

"Think soberly; keep chaste; work at home; show kindness?"

There is Mr. C, whose wife is a much-publicized "screwball" who acts first and thinks later — if she thinks at all;

There is Mr. D, who *everybody knows* puts up with an openly immoral wife;

There is Mr. E, who can never invite a friend to visit or a boss to dine because his gad-about wife never turns a hand in their pig-sty home;

There is Mr. F, whose wife's mean disposition and malicious deeds have alienated both their families, made them no new friends, and reduced him to the status of a martyred midget in only *one blissful year!*

"Obey their own husbands?" There is Mr. G, who must beg his wife's pardon for asking her permission to seek her approval before taking a breath! Mrs. G has run her husband's life since the day they were married, and she has made a *botch* of it! In her determination to make her husband an important man, a person of authority in business, an elder in the church, and a pillar in the community, she has made him, instead, just one more miserable Walter Mitty in a long procession of hilariously hen-pecked husbands!

While the Mesdames A through G, and their counterparts, are hurting their husbands, they are actually hurting themselves more. Each such wife, by her own belittling behavior, is damaging the reputation, diminishing the prestige, and destroying the effectiveness of the man upon whom her own reputation, prestige, and effectiveness depends. The worst hurt to herself is the solemn responsibility she must bear throughout eternity for causing the Word of God to be blasphemed.

When a man marries the right woman, she becomes Exhibit A-Plus, the most convincing proof of his Success. Her own good life brings glory and honor to her husband, herself, and her God. To such a woman, it seems such an *easy* way to accomplish *so much*:

> Because I love you
> And love our children enough to give them myself,
> Because I love you

And am discreet,
Because I love you
And love our home enough to keep it clean and comfortable,
Because I love you
And show kindness to others,
Because I love you
Enough to love to obey your every word,
There are, my dear, these three
On whom all men will speak well:
  You — my husband,
  God — our Heavenly Father,
  And Me — Who love both.
       — L. T.

VII

Leading Our Little Ones

L ONG ago, a humble, God-fearing woman heard the thrilling announcement, "You're going to have a baby!" Immediately, both she and her husband asked God for guidance. "How shall we order the child?" (Judges 13:12).

Before one is blessed with offspring, he may speak of rearing children — plural — training *children*. Parents of more than one child soon discover that each child is singular — an individual. Each has his own special personality and his own special needs, which parents must somehow manage to meet if that child is to grow up and develop into all that he could become to the glory of God.

There are, however, some basic needs which are common to all children everywhere. "How shall we order the child?" can be answered in part by supplying the necessities of life, as the material needs are called. It can be answered more emphatically by showering him with gifts — *enduring gifts.* If you would give your child a guarantee of happiness, consider these gifts that money cannot buy, that you can bestow only by your careful teaching and example, and without which your child will be poor indeed:

The Gift of Thankfulness. Look around you. Who are the happy people? Are they not the thankful people? I am convinced they are happy because they are thankful, rather than thankful because they are happy! Had they waited upon "happiness" before knowing "gratitude," they should be waiting still, and in vain. For it is the vibrant force of a thankful heart that gives life to joy, and keeps it breathing, even in the presence of death.

Surely it is apparent to most adults that if one is to be happy at all, in this life, it must be in spite of much that is unpleasant, even downright tragic. And the magic ingredient, the wonder drug, that makes happiness possible amid such surroundings is thankfulness. So, in leading our little ones, we want to give them the enduring gift of thankfulness.

But how? By cultivating in our own lives the attitude of gratitude. Our children know if we have it, and they know if we haven't it, by what we say and what we do. We should not minimize the importance of either, for though our actions do sometimes belie our words, words are important too, in expressing gratitude. The parent who feels thankful, says so, and shows it, is not likely to fail. Children of such parents receive daily instruction in the fine art of happiness.

Recently, a neighbor said, "You know, ever so often I find myself thinking about *next time*, as if I were going through this life again. Next time I'll do this, next time I'll do that." She always felt a little shock, she said, to realize that there would be no "next time." She expressed a subconscious attitude which is at the bottom of much ingratitude and consequent unhappiness: *We take too much for granted.*

Perhaps our neighbor has read the poem that expresses the sobering truth, "I shall not pass this way again." Remembering "this is *it*" compels us to fill our days fuller, *now;* to enjoy people, things, life, *now!* When we stop taking time for granted, we rejoice at the glorious possibilities of each moment.

Isn't it a hateful thing, to take one of the fresh, unused days that God presents us every morning and ruin it, grumbling? "The weather isn't right." "The scenery isn't much." "The people aren't friendly." "I have to work." Such mouthings come from hearts that are taking for granted the greatest blessing of all — life itself.

What of the mother who whines, "I detest grocery shopping. So much trouble to put them away! How I hate to cook them!" Can she expect her children to believe her when she *says* her *thank-you prayers* at the table?

One little boy probably did not deserve the rebuke he received from his father when he thanked the Lord that "Mama finally got the dinner on the table." At least he could feel thankful, and say so.

Children who grow up in homes where Daddy can say "Thank you" to Mother for such ordinary things as a hot meal, an ironed shirt, a clean house, and Mother can say "Thank you" to Daddy for such everyday things as a fresh-mowed lawn, a fresh-swept car, fresh-painted steps — these children are more likely to say "Thank you" to Mother and Daddy for the ordinary, everyday gifts of an extra-special love.

Where both parents are quick to express sincere gratitude to friends, relatives, employers, employees — not because it's etiquette, but because it's *pleasant* — children will inherit the marvelous capacity for happiness that is gratitude's own gift to the grateful heart.

That inspired man of long ago was giving us a formula for happiness as modern as today's mother, when he wrote, "In everything give thanks . . ."

From "The Happiest Gift," by Lois Terry, *THE CHRISTIAN MOTHER*, Spring, 1964. Reprinted by permission.

The Gift of Truthfulness. "One of the saddest experiences of my career," a junior high school teacher related, "was to work with a twelve-year-old boy who had already established himself as such a notorious liar that he could not make his teachers, classmates, principal, or parents believe him, even when he was telling the truth!" If a lying tongue is an abomination unto the Lord, it is also a curse to its owner. Parents who can instill in their children a love for truth are giving them one of the greatest of all gifts. How can we do it?

When a child psychologist was asked, "Why do children tell lies?" her answer was a shocking one to parents. A child usually learns to lie through the influence of his parents. He copies their example. She called on mothers and fathers to examine their own truthfulness.

Do you make promises that are never kept?

Do you threaten punishments that are never carried out?

Do you tell your child to say you're not in when it's inconvenient to talk to the neighbor on the phone?

Do you say, "I don't have any money," when your billfold is bulging and the blind broom-peddler knocks on the door?

Do you ask the operator to clear the party line for an "emergency" call every time your child wants to talk to his cousin?

After a series of such experiences, your child may begin taking care of himself in the way you have taught him: by telling stories. You can lecture him without end that honesty is the best policy, but he knows that you don't believe it — because you don't practice it.

A long time ago, William Shakespeare put some good strong words into the mouth of a parent named Polonius — words of advice to his son:

> This above all: to thine own self be true;
> And it must follow, as the night the day,
> Thou cans't not then be false to any man.

There is still no better advice around, for young and old alike. For, to "Buy the truth and sell it not" (Prov. 23:23) makes possible what Charles W. Eliot has called "one of the purest and most enduring of human pleasures . . . the possession of a good name among one's neighbors and acquaintances."* This is the happiness of which Solomon spoke: "A good name is rather to be chosen than great riches . . ." (Prov. 22:1).

Parents — even wealthy parents — cannot buy a good name for their children. They can bestow it only by setting an example of truthfulness before them at all times and in every place. It is a worthy gift, carrying with it a life-

---

*From *THE DURABLE SATISFACTIONS OF LIFE*, Thomas Y. Crowell Company, publishers.

time guarantee of happiness, straight from the Word of God:

> For he that will love life and see good
> days, let him refrain his tongue from evil,
> and his lips that they speak no guile.
>
> — I Peter 3:10

The Gift of Time. This may seem a strange bequest. But children do need time — to be children! Why is it, then, that many parents are cheating their children? In a recent women's magazine, a physician accused Americans of being so busy *doing* that we hardly have time to *think*. We are depriving our children of the chance to develop their creative resources. We allow them little time to think.

Sherry's case is typical. She is nine years old, and she has been given every advantage: piano lessons, fencing instructions, girl-scout meetings, drama classes. Sherry has need of nothing — except time. She has no time to dream, to reflect, to wonder. She must, instead, be always working, always doing, always accomplishing. Her parents see to that.

Victor Hugo wrote: "A man is not idle because he is absorbed in thought. There is visible labor and there is invisible labor." The same is true for a child. When his creative thoughts are interrupted, he loses his chance to explore his own resources, to observe the wonders under his nose, to figure out a solution to some puzzle he may have discovered. These activities are as important to his development as are the endless hours of regimented programs with which well-meaning parents pressure their children.

Through patience, and love for the child, parents can allow him the luxury of idle times — times for introspection and reverie. It is an enduring gift: vital to the child's creative growth, essential to the development of a rich personality, and often the springboard to true accomplishment.

The Gift of Faith. This is the greatest gift you could desire for your child. Religious faith, which is founded on the Word of God.

Faith cannot be feigned. It cannot be hidden. Your child knows if you have it — by how you act. Without faith in God, a child is severely handicapped. He has no real incentive toward righteousness, no resistance to evil, no purpose in life. At best, his life might be described as ". . . a wave of the sea, driven with the wind and tossed . . . ." (Jas. 1:6).

Every child born into this world deserves the most godly mother and father this world can give him. For he has been born into *God's world.* God is his Creator. God will sustain him all of his days. God will judge him in the Judgment. It is the solemn duty of every parent to bring up each child in "the nurture and admonition of the Lord." This is the language of Ephesians 6:4. Faith cannot be bought; it must be taught.

As loving parents, leading our little ones, let us give them the gift of faith. It will endure, even unto that day when we shall stand with them before our Heavenly Father, saying with indescribable gladness and gratitude, "Behold, here are *we*, Lord, and the children Thou gavest *us.*"

VIII

She Walks in Beauty

A LITTLE girl was discussing two of her teachers: "Mrs. Brown wears nice clothes and *looks* pretty. But Mrs. Day smiles, and doesn't talk mean to the janitors, and even cares how we feel. Mrs. Day's *beautiful!*" The child's words illustrate an axiom which has been handed down from mother to daughter for generations: "Beauty *is* as beauty *does.*" And, while Mrs. Brown's husband may congratulate himself on his wife's good looks and good taste in dress, it is Mrs. Day's husband who can go home each evening to a truly beautiful wife. For experience reveals what the Scriptures teach: true beauty is an inner beauty, a loveliness of mind from which spring unselfish deeds and uplifting dispositions. Beauty *does,* so beauty *is.*

This does not mean that the outward appearance is unimportant. It would be an unloving woman, indeed, who would not want to look as attractive as she possibly could for the man she married. It would be an unfeeling husband who would not be pleased to call an outwardly beautiful woman, "My wife." *To keep myself lovely to look at* is one of the promises every wife should make to herself on behalf of the man she loves.

But, a more sacred promise, by far, is *to make myself lovely to live with.* "She walks in beauty" who develops the spiritual comeliness which honors her husband as no outward prettiness could.

A truly beautiful character can be seen in the stunning portrait, painted by a renowned artist, the apostle Peter, with the Holy Spirit guiding his brush. The picture hangs in the Great Gallery of Masterpieces, the Holy Bible, for all to see, admire, and emulate. The viewer is struck by the radiant personality it depicts (I Pet. 3:3,4; II Pet. 1:5-7).

Beautiful Clothing. ". . . whose adorning let it not be that outward adorning of plaiting the hair and of wearing of gold, or of putting on of apparel. But let it be that hidden man of the heart, in that which is not corruptible, even the ornament of a meek and quiet spirit, which is in the sight of God of great price" (I Pet. 3:3,4).

A prominent psychologist said, "The best-dressed woman is not the woman whose dress everyone admires, but the woman who is so well-dressed that people are aware only of her personality, not of her clothes." Times and conditions may change, hoop-skirts may give way to mini-skirts and hobbles to tents, but the meek and quiet spirit will never go out of style. She who walks in beauty by the side of her husband will be wearing the high-priced, high fashion ornament which God has designed and named.

"Meek and quiet spirit" — what does it mean? Not mousey. Gentle, yes, but strong. Strong within. Meekness is a fruit of power. Jesus was meek; He had all the resources of God at His command. He did not have to lash out at the world, assert Himself, plunge from pinnacles of elation to caverns of despair. Strong within, he could be strong without.

Jesus' strength within can give his followers that same tranquility of spirit, so pleasant to possess, so beautiful to behold, so lovely to live with. A meek and quiet spirit will neither deliberately provoke others, nor be easily provoked by others. He who is blessed with such a wife will have to forego certain "pleasures" which other men have to endure: nagging, needling, quarreling, recriminations, pouting, sulking, fault-finding, retaliations! — and such like! He will, instead, be "forced" to stroll through life with his well-dressed wife by his side — his wife, gorgeously arrayed in her meek and quiet spirit.

Along with this inner beauty of spirit, the artist has painted other striking features. Each one contributes to each of the others, and complements the whole, in the creation of a beautiful character. Every truly beautiful woman will possess these beautiful features:

Beautiful Figure. The portrait begins with a perfect physique. A spiritually solid foundation, well able to support and enhance the other attractive features. The apostle's picture of beauty *begins with faith* from which the other characteristics spring. "And besides this, give all diligence to add to your faith . . . ." (II Pet. 1:5).

It is impossible to please God without faith (Heb. 11:6). It is also impossible, without faith, to develop true beauty of character. For faith, which comes by ". . . hearing . . . the word of God" (Rom. 10:17), becomes a sound and sure basis for all actions and reactions. Since faith is the "substance of things hoped for, the evidence of things not seen" (Heb. 11:1), it furnishes a forward-looking, optimistic approach to every day, as it provides a solid foundation on which to build an effective, happy, and beautiful life. A lovely character, without faith, is as unlikely as a face without a body.

Beautiful Feet. "Add to your faith, virtue . . ." (v. 5). It was Cinderella's Prince Charming who searched every house in his father's kingdom to find the beautiful foot that could fit the tiny glass slipper. In real life, perhaps, pretty feet are not as universally admired as pretty eyes or pretty hair; but, in the portrait of a beautiful character, one might visualize the first addition as feet. For virtue is another word for courage and moral energy: the courage to walk with Christ; the energy to follow wherever He leads. The firm, sure step of Christ is the finest example of virtue.

With added virtue, a wife keeps herself pure in mind, pure in body, forbidding all evil thoughts and harmful habits to enter the sacred temple of her spiritual house. With virtue, also, she guards her earthly home from all destructive elements, saying, "Make not my husband's house a den of thieves!" to any and all who would steal the precious peace, wholesome joy, and loving oneness of her family.

Virtue's feet stand firm when they stand right; step forward boldly when the need is great; step backward only to retract a step, rescue a friend, or renew a vow. She who walks on virtue's feet can stand still — even when mocked, and cursed, and spit upon. Can stand still, as Jesus did, and pray, ". . . Father, forgive them . . ." (Lk. 23:34). True beauty includes virtue.

Beautiful Head. In grandmother's day, the shape of a new baby's head was carefully observed and often discussed. A well-shaped head, everybody knew, meant a "pretty baby." Earlier, the Greeks who idolized physical beauty, placed great emphasis on the contour of the brow, nose, chin, and cheek bones. Even in today's fashion world, interesting bone structure is the most essential feature for a successful modeling career.

The beautiful model in Peter's famous portrait has an admirable head. "Add to your . . . virtue knowledge . . ." (v. 5).

A person who possessed faith and courage without knowledge would be as dangerous as a body and feet without a head. If the portrait should omit its head, it would be a monstrosity: a creature without knowledge, possessing feet that would run bravely in any direction, never really knowing which way it was going. She who walks in beauty, after the likeness of the portrait, will be diligent in her study of the Bible, earnestly desiring to grow in knowledge.

Beautiful Lips. This feature can suggest self-control, or temperance. "Add to your . . . knowledge temperance . . ." (v. 5). A truly beautiful woman speaks according to one unfailing formula: "Let your speech be always with grace [kindness] seasoned with salt [taste-appeal, helpfulness]" (Col. 4:6). *Always.* Nothing passes her lips that cannot be said in kindness, in good taste, and out of a genuinely helpful spirit.

Where does that leave harsh criticism? Malicious gossip? Profane utterances? Dirty jokes? Deliberate lies? Self-centered babblings? Angry outbursts? James emphasized the obvious when he reasoned, in Jas. 3, that anyone who can control his tongue will be able to control his whole body. And every woman can verify a further observation: a wife who can control her tongue at home, with her husband, her children, and her *telephone* has nothing to fear from the outside world!

The man who marries a temperate wife will not have to be embarassed and annoyed by her excesses. She will neither eat herself into oblivion, nor starve herself into extinction. She will sometimes be able to pass up the "bargain" she sees in the store window. She will seldom lose her temper before his friends, and never tell off his boss! She may not always be a poised, well-balanced, perfect example of self-control in the presence of her husband and children, but *she will always be trying to be.* ". . . giving all diligence . . . to add temperance."

Beautiful Eyes. To see and appreciate God's wonderful world and all the wonderful people in it. To see afar off, beyond the horizon of here and now. "Exercise your self-control to develop patience" (v. 6, Amplified New Testament). "Add to your . . . temperance . . ." Eyes of patience can see what other eyes cannot: the importance of waiting. "Rest in the Lord, and wait patiently for him . . ." (Psalms 37:7). Patient eyes can see some gain, some growth, some good in hardships, disappointments, and suffering. "We glory in tribulation knowing that tribulation worketh patience" (Rom. 5:3).

Patient eyes look often to Jesus for patience without a flaw. He was patient with friends, patient with enemies, patient in pain, patient unto death. Every day He faced misunderstanding, ingratitude, criticism, and abuse; yet, the end of every day found him just as gentle and uncomplaining as at the dawn. How, then, could one who claims to know God go about whining, with a chip on her shoulders? Patient eyes can see the need to practice His patience, so that those close and dear to her can be drawn closer to Him by beholding her own "beautiful eyes" of patience.

Beautiful Ears. "Add to your . . . patience godliness . . ."
v. 6). Godliness is reverence — a God-hearing, God-fearing disposition. In the portrait of Christian character, godliness might be represented by ears that are open to all of God's instructions.

She who walks in beauty knows that reverence for God is not a Sunday hat that can be put on or laid off; if she appears godly on Sunday and not on Monday, then her Sunday's reverence was a sham. She does not have to say it aloud — her husband and her children know full well that with her, every day is the Lord's day! Her reverence for God is another of the lovely characteristics that make her so truly beautiful.

Beautiful Hands. "Add to your . . . godliness brotherly kindness . . ." (v. 7). The portrait of a Christian would not be complete without hands to minister to the needs of others. To hide its arms and hands would be to present an unbearably selfish person. Brotherly kindness requires a readiness to render help to those close by. In another passage, Paul instructs Christians to be kind, tender-hearted, and forgiving (Eph. 4:32). Brotherly kindness includes compassion and forgiveness.

Beautiful Arms. To embrace the whole world, for whom Christ died. With a final bold stroke, "Add . . . love" (v. 7), the portrait is finished. Love is, in reality, the expression of the whole personality, the outstanding attribute of a beautiful Christian character, motivating all that one does. It is a perfect picture — the character that started with faith, now completed through love. And what is the relationship of faith and love in the Scriptures? ". . . faith . . . worketh by love" (Gal. 5:6). Love is the sum total of a beautiful Christian character.

TO ONE WHO WOULD BE BEAUTIFUL:

They say that you're in love with love,
I hope it's true!
For could you find a finer hinge
To fasten your heart to?

Love-lovers look for *good*,
And hold it tight;
Love-lovers cling to *praise*,
Embracing *right*.

So you who build your life on love
Will have no part
To hug your hatred, pet your peeves,
Nor woo your wounded heart.

Love-lovers look like God:
"Born from above";
Love-lovers love like God:
"For God *is* love."

So never fall *in love with hate;*
Nor *out* with *love*, I pray,
And God, Himself in love with love,
Will bless your every day!

— L. T.

She walks in beauty who walks in love. Love big enough to include her husband, her children, her neighbor, her God. Love strong enough to give all diligence to add to her faith, virtue, knowledge, temperance, patience, godliness, brotherly kindness, and ever *more love*.

IX

His Heiress Wife

THE daughter of a multimillionaire, only heir to her father's fabulous empire, marries an honest, hard-working mechanic, and headlines scream, "*Oil* heiress elopes with *grease* monkey!" Even when the heir to a fortune from *glue* gets himself permanently attached to an heiress whose money's in *mud*, it makes the front page. Heiresses' weddings are considered "good copy."

Yet, whenever and wherever a man takes a wife, he marries an heiress — if both partners are Christians. Newspapers might announce, quite truthfully, "Bill Jones and Mary Smith become 'heirs together of the grace of life.'"

> . . . . ye husbands, dwell with them,
> according to knowledge, giving honour unto
> the wife, as unto the weaker vessel, and
> as being heirs together of the grace of life;
> that your prayers be not hindered.
>
> — I Peter 1:3-7

The apostle wrote this instruction to husbands following his admonition to wives to be in subjection. The man is reminded that, while his wife may be his inferior physically, she is his equal spiritually. They are co-inheritors of the grace — God's unmerited favor — of life. The wife is reminded of the fortune she stands to inherit with her husband. And both are reminded of their need to pray.

What is it that a Christian wife inherits with her Christian husband which was not already hers without him? The answer is *nothing* — and the answer is *everything*. Nothing that was not already promised; yet, everything she had coming to her as a Christian will be coming up *double*, as a Christian's wife.

Double Life. Or, to be more exact, a doubly good life! The Christian life is a way of life, and it is the best way to live, whether or not it is lived with a husband. Jesus said of all people, ". . . I am come that they might have life, and that they might have it more abundantly" (Jno. 10:10). But, while two may not be able to live as *cheaply* as one, they can certainly live more *fully*.

A woman may sing, "It's a good life, to be free, and face the unknown!" but she doesn't really believe it. The good life, as every woman knows, is not free but securely tied down, inseparably bound to one man, and facing not the unknown, but the very well-known: her husband's dear familiar face, her children's dear familiar smiles, her house's old familiar warmth. The Christian wife's pleasures are doubly precious when she shares with her Christian husband and fellow-heir.

But, to "double your pleasure, double your fun," is not her chief aim in life. There is, also, the greater and ever-present purpose — to win others for Christ. "Saved to save" is as true of the Twentieth Century woman as it was of the First Century disciples. She who marries a Christian rejoices that she can double her influence.

Double Light. If the Source of all light could say to each disciple, "Ye are the light of the world. A city that is set on a hill cannot be hid" (Matt. 5:14), how dazzling is the radiance of a really good marriage! A Christian wife has more than doubled her opportunities to let her light shine; therefore, she has an equally increased obligation to "maintain good works" (Titus 3:8).

For God who has joined *one wife* to *one husband* has as inseparably joined one's *influence* and one's *good works*. "Let your light so shine before men, that they may see your good works, and glorify your Father which is in Heaven" (Matt. 5:15). It is by the light of her good works that God is glorified and others attracted to Christ. The power of such influence has been described by John Greenleaf Whittier:

> The dear Lord's best interpreters
> Are humble human souls;
> The gospel of a life like His
> Is more than book or scrolls.
>
> From scheme and creed the light goes out,
> The saintly fact survives;
> The blessed Master none can doubt,
> Revealed in holy lives.

When each marriage partner recognizes his own individual responsibility, and both rejoice in the privilege of being "laborers together with God" (I Cor. 3:9), the world about them cannot but be made brighter and brought closer to Heaven by the intensity of their double light.

Double Prayer. The heritage of double-strength prayer may seem of little significance, since the "effectual fervent" prayer of *one* righteous person "availeth much" (Jas. 5:16). Yet, Jesus did teach that there is strength in numbers:

> Again I say unto you that if two of you
> shall agree on earth as touching anything
> that they shall ask, it shall be done for them
> of my Father which is in Heaven.
>
> For where two or three are gathered to-
> gether in my name, there am I in the midst
> of them.
>
> — Matthew 18:19,20

While two can approach God's throne with double assurance, Peter's instructions to husbands (I Pet. 1:3-7) must
be taken as a warning that prayers can be hindered if the
husband fails to show his wife the consideration which is
due her.   In Peter's words there is an understated but un-
mistakable reminder of the poverty within a home which
is without the wealth of prayer.   There is, also, a joyous
implication of the wealth within that home which possesses
the privilege of unhindered prayer.

No single blessing of their "togetherness" can quite equal
the Christian couple's togetherness in prayer.   When two
hearts, beating as one, beat a path to the Father's door,
to praise Him, to petition Him, and to thank Him for the
privilege of such double-rich moments, they achieve a closeness with which nothing on earth can compare.   It can
only be described as Heavenly.   Their lives will be a source
of blessing to all the lives they touch.   Their burdens will
seem less burdensome; their problems less puzzling. Their
hearts will be guarded, their home surrounded, by the comforting strength of their combined prayers.

Double Crown. Among her wedding gifts, every new
bride receives towels, pillow cases, or other items monogrammed "His" and "Hers."   The gifts never fail to pro-
duce a squeal of delight!   How much more delightful is the

Christian wife's discovery that there are gifts of great price in the Lord's Lay-Away: identical gifts, labeled "His" and "Hers!"

> . . . Henceforth there is laid up for me a crown of righteousness. — I Timothy 4:8
>
> . . . Ye shall receive a crown of glory that fadeth not away. — I Peter 5:4
>
> . . . Be thou faithful unto death, and I will give thee a crown of life. — Revelation 2:10
>
> . . . heirs together of the grace of life . . . — I Peter 1:7

Although there will be two individual rewards, each partner must participate in the winning of both. For, should one partner fail, both crowns may well be lost. As with the monogrammed towels, there is *one* for each, but *both* are theirs; each owns half of the other's crown. ". . . heirs together . . ." of eternal life: *His, Hers, Theirs!*

Is this not a double incentive for doubling efforts? While she is enjoying the good, abundant life now, the wife must see that the regular deposits are made on the treasures she has in lay-away. In the Lord's plan, payments are as easy as they are beneficial: regular worship, regular service to others, and consistent Christian living, all motivated always by love. God's very requirements are also God's richest blessings.

The knowledge of two crowns laid up in Heaven ought to impress each would-be-wearer with his responsibility for the other's soul. In this closest of all earthly relationships, there is always danger of a false sense of security: "It's all right, because we agree that it is!" "It can't be wrong, because we both enjoy it!" "It isn't really necessary, because we don't seem to need it!" How terrible is the thought that two who have loved each other "with the breath, smiles, tears of all their lives" might allow that very love to cause them, through carelessness or through selfishness, to lose their souls. How thrilling is the thought that two who have so loved might also so live that "if God choose, they shall but love each other better after death." Heirs together of the grace of life — through all eternity.

The hope of such an inheritance continues to bless the partner who is left when one is taken in death. Each day takes on added meaning and beauty, because it is a day to be lived well, in preparation for all the beautiful days to come: days to be together with the Lord — for always.

Double life, double light, double prayer, double crown — these are some of the double blessings which the Christian wife of a Christian husband inherits. Is it any wonder she often feels far wealthier than all the heiresses to all the fortunes of all the world? With the lowly boy who became a king, she can declare, "We shall not want!"

X

How Much Am I Worth?

THE book of Proverbs has been called "A divine handbook on the conduct of life . . ." In it, a young man of marriageable age can hear God say:

> Who can find a virtuous [worthy, A. S. V.] woman? for her price is far above rubies.
>
> — Proverbs 31:10

Such a woman exists. She has lived for centuries on the pages of God's Word and in the lives of countless women who have found the "virtuous woman" an inspiration and a challenge. Because of her, women everywhere, regardless of circumstance, can dare to "think big" — can aspire to become women of virtue, worthy of praise, and worth more than money to their husbands. Yet, this model wife's existence actually began in the words of a wise mother to her young son. King Lemuel declares in Proverbs 31:1 that the description of an ideal wife was "taught him" by his mother.

Although the Holy Spirit breathed these words long ago, they are as up-to-date as the daily newspaper. Times and customs may have changed, but God's principles are changeless. The queen mother's picture of female excellence can still help a prospective bridegroom to know what to look for in choosing a wife. It can still help a prospective bride to know what God calls a *good* wife. It can still help every wife to answer the very personal question, "Am *I* a *good* wife?"

The truth is, not all wives are. Good wives, like "a good man" are sometimes "hard to find!" The need to *search* for such a woman is indicated by the question, ". . . who can find? . ." A good marriage is never an accident.

When the search is ended, and the good wife is finally found, that man who is privileged to have her by his side possesses "something of value," indeed. Every woman who is ambitious to be of real value to her husband can profit by examining herself in the light of this valuable woman's life. *By answering honestly certain simple questions about herself, she can discover the answer to the big question: "How much am I worth?"*

AM I TRUSTWORTHY?. YES............ NO............

"The heart of her husband doth safely trust in her, so that he shall have no need of spoil" (v. 11). Some kings went into battle to gain spoil for their households, but the worthy woman's husband is not driven to desperation to dangerous and dishonest methods. Because his wife is at home, on-the-job, he has no cause to worry or be anxious. He can put his mind at east, knowing that she will be honest, in every respect.

Honest With Time — the most expensive commodity on earth, and the least appreciated. A husband who is hoping "to succeed in business *with* really trying," has a right to hope for as much from his wife. A trustworthy wife will be honest in the wise use of her time.

Honest With Money. Since the wife buys everything from groceries and clothing to medicines and amusements for her family, she has chosen herself a career in the field of economics, whether she meant to or not. The husband of a worthy woman can risk his wife's judgment, can depend upon her truthfulness, can turn household matters over to her and forget them. She will be honest in the wise spending of their money.

Honest With the Children. God gave man a help meet because he has to have somebody. Because he has her, he can go off to work every morning knowing that the children God gave them will be treated fairly and tenderly. He can depend upon his wife to see that they are trained to respect God, to love their parents, and to mind their manners, even when he must be away.

Honest With Her Husband. "She doeth him good and not evil all the days of her life" (v. 12). Her marriage vows will be held sacred until death separates them.

The good wife is trustworthy: honest with time, honest with money, honest with the children, honest with her husband. Am I?

AM I INDUSTRIOUS? YES............ NO............

"She seeketh wool, and flax, and worketh willingly with her hands" (v. 13). The woman whom God calls *worthy* is a *worker*. By working willingly, with a heart full of gratitude that she can work, she proves her love for her husband and her children. The whiner, the complainer, the self-pitier cannot measure up. The lazy wife is a disgrace, not a jewel.

A lady psychologist who spent several years interviewing marriage experts has concluded that former secretaries and nurses make the best wives. Among her reasons, she lists: they know how to run the show while playing second fiddle; they know how to forgive all insults; they know how to be thankful for not having to work eight hours a day. While her opinion includes some good lessons for every wife to learn, it is interesting to see "the luxury of a shorter working day" among the good things a good wife appreciates. For, according to the One who cannot be wrong, the ideal wife especially appreciates work. Working willingly with her hands, seeking ever more work, she seems not to covet the luxury of an eight-hour day. The good wife is industrious. Am I?

AM I THRIFTY? YES............ NO............

"She is like the merchant ships, she bringeth her bread from afar" (v. 14). Today's woman is "like the merchant ships" when she makes the very best use of every dollar, wasting nothing.

Jesus teaches thrift, not stinginess. He taught men to save, not hoard. He wasted nothing, but he gave bushels of food away (Matt. 14:15-21; 15:32-38). While a good wife is not concerned with laying up treasures on earth (Matt. 6:19-21), her family can have more to give, more to use as God intended, more treasures in Heaven, because she is thrifty. Am I?

AM I BOTH ENERGETIC AND SYSTEMATIC?
YES............ NO............

"She riseth also while it is yet night, and giveth meat to her household, and a portion [their task, A.S.V.] to her maidens." A woman worth "far above rubies" has to get an early start! She must plan and prepare well-balanced meals for all those whose bodies are in her care, balancing the budget while she balances the diet. Sometimes this, in itself, seems an impossible task. "I can do one or the other," a new bride said, "but both at the same time — that would take an Einstein!" She must be organized, giving each child some share of responsibility, even though, at first, it may seem more of a hindrance than a help. A good wife's family will be both well-fed and well-trained because she is energetic and systematic. Am I?

ARE MY OUTSIDE INTERESTS ALWAYS PRODUCTIVE?
      YES............ NO............

"She considereth a field and buyeth it; with the fruit of her hands she planteth a vineyard" (v. 16). This good wife's outside interests were creative ones, combining real-estate with agriculture. The results were beneficial to her family. The worthy woman has no interest in time-consuming activities that take her away from her family and serve no useful purpose. When a good wife develops an interest outside her home, it will be with her family's welfare in mind; it will be a productive one. Is mine?

DO I TAKE GOOD CARE OF MY OWN HEALTH?
      YES............ NO............

"She girdeth her loins with strength, and strengtheneth her arms" (v. 17). There is no virtue in wrecking one's own health in the process of protecting another's. The worthy woman makes a conscious effort to be strong physically. Knowing her body to be the temple of God, she aims to glorify God in her body, as well as in her spirit (I Cor. 5:19-21).

Today's wife and mother sometimes seems to be trying to cross a *dozen* bridges before she has found her way to *one.* The mental tensions and exhausting routines of daily living often result in actual illness. Psychiatrists say that much sickness is a means of escaping responsibilities.

What is the answer? The wise wife knows it: courage. She must develop the courage to live simply, to say *no* to some things, to forget about what the Joneses do, to remember what Christ would have her do: "... be content ..." (Philippians 4:11; Luke 3:14; I Tim. 6:8; Heb. 13:5).

A calm, quiet spirit is a great aid toward physical fitness — as necessary as these other essentials: proper diet, adequate rest, daily exercise, regular physical examinations, and medical attention when it is needed.

A good wife gives thanks for such strength as she has, by taking good care of her body. Do I?

DO I TAKE PLEASURE IN DOING MY WORK WELL?
YES............ NO............

"She perceiveth that her merchandise is good: her candle goeth not out by night. She layeth her hands to the spindle, and her hands hold the distaff" (vv. 18,19). It is one thing to be a worker, and another thing to be a conscientious worker. A worthy woman knows the joy that comes from a job well done. The happiness she receives from such an accomplishment makes up for all the candles she has burned in the effort. Because her enthusiasm remains at an all-time high, the worthy woman keeps her production at its peak, and her quality consistently superior. A good wife need not be ashamed of her work. Am I?

AM I CHARITABLE? YES............ NO............

"She stretcheth out her hand to the poor; yea, she reacheth forth her hands to the needy" (v. 20). No good woman was ever satisfied to lavish all her strength and wealth on her own household. Nor has she ever been satisfied in helping only those poor who come asking for her assistance. A good wife does some *stretching* and *reaching*. She seeks out the poor and needy, in order to help them. Do I?

DO I GET THINGS DONE ON TIME? YES............ NO............

"She is not afraid of the snow for her household: for all her household are clothed with scarlet" (v. 21). The worthy woman does not wait until the snows come to get ready for winter. Her theme song might be, "Let it snow, let it snow, let it snow!"

The modern billboard signs, "THINK" and "PLAN AHEAD" might have been written with housewives in mind. The husband of Mrs. Put-it-off and the children of Mother Dilly Dally may have to go hungry, be cold, look unkempt, suffer disappointments, because their wife and mother cannot or will not learn to start early enough to finish on time. By trying to make things *easy on herself*, she makes life *harder* on both her family and herself. A good wife is not a procrastinator. Am I?

DO I KEEP BOTH MYSELF AND OUR HOME NEAT AND
    ATTRACTIVE? YES............ NO............

"She maketh herself coverings of tapestry; her clothing is silk and purple" (v. 22). A wife who loves God will want her home to reflect His appreciation for "all things bright and beautiful."

Beauty is *not* synonymous with *elaborateness*, nor dependent upon *extravagance*. A wife can be sweet, and carefully groomed, with her love of beauty expressed in such simple things as a becoming housedress, made by her own busy hands.

A good wife is "so nice to come home to," because she keeps both herself and her home attractive. Do I?

DO I HELP MY HUSBAND TO HAVE A GOOD REPUTA-
TION? YES............ NO............

"Her husband is known in the gates, when he sitteth among the elders of the land" (v. 23). Because a worthy woman is careful, discreet, wise, and helpful, her husband can serve his community, his city, his country. He does not have to fear such taunts as, "First, clean up the mess in your own house!"

A good wife cherisheth the good name of her husband. Even though the Bible's worthy woman entered actively into the business world of her day — "She maketh fine linen, and selleth it; and delivereth girdles unto the merchant" (v. 24) — she seems to have conducted herself so becomingly that her husband's prestige was in no way threatened.

A good wife is always a help, never a hindrance, to her husband's reputation. Am I?

DO I APPEAR POISED, DIGNIFIED, AND HAPPY?
    YES............ NO............

"Strength and honour [dignity, A.S.V.] are her clothing; and she shall rejoice in time to come" (v. 25). Strength of character and dignity of manner come from knowing right, and doing right. A worthy woman will not be attracted by every silly fad and foolish fashion. These are the outward trappings of the inwardly insecure. Calm assurance and gentle refinement must come from within. They cannot be affected or pretended.

> She may safely wear elegant garments, who in character and bearing is elegant without their aid. If honor be your clothing, the suit will last a lifetime, but if clothing be your honor, it will soon be worn threadbare.
>
> — Arnot

A good husband has a right to expect more than a frantic fashion fanatic for a wife. He deserves a good wife — one who is poised, dignified, and obviously happy. Am I?

DO I THINK BEFORE I SPEAK? YES............ NO............

"She openeth her mouth with wisdom; and in her tongue is the law of kindness" (v. 26). The worthy woman must be a praying woman, for, according to James 1:5, wisdom may be obtained through prayer. Only by constant prayer can one acquire the wisdom to speak *wisely* and *kindly*.

The husband and children of a worthy woman do not have to be satisfied with an occasional worthwhile thought, an occasional kind word, from their wife and mother. She seems not to open her mouth at all, except with wisdom, and not to speak at all, unless she can speak according to her own law of kindness.

A good wife will pray for wisdom, and cultivate kindness. She will think before she speaks. Do I?

Verse 31 summarizes and re-emphasizes the dedicated life of the woman who is worth "more than rubies" to her family. "She looketh well to the ways of her household, and eateth not the bread of idleness." And, what is the thanks she gets? "Her children arise up, and call her blessed; her husband also, and he praiseth her."

DO I OFTEN RECEIVE COMPLIMENTS FROM MY CHIL-
DREN AND PRAISE FROM MY HUSBAND?
YES............. NO.............

As a funeral tribute to a good wife, mother, and grand-mother, the preacher read the thirty-first chapter of Proverbs without comment. The bereaved husband listened, with bowed head. At the end of each verse, he whispered a fervent, "Amen!" To him, the preacher was describing in detail the beloved wife who had been, for half-a-century, by his side. What finer tribute could any woman wish?

Now, for the *big* question:

AM I A GOOD WIFE? YES............. NO.............

If and when a wife can manage, with God's help, to answer "Yes' to all the questions included in this chapter, prosperity and praise are promised her. Because she is a valuable asset to the man she married, God says of her, "Give her of the fruit of her hands; and let her own works praise her in the gates" (v. 31).

XI

To Live Together

Will you take this man to be your
wedded husband, to live together . . . ?

EVERY bride is asked this question first. It precedes all
other questions in the marriage ceremony. Her single
"I will," promises much:

I will love him;
I will obey him;
I will comfort him;
I will honor and keep him;
I will keep myself only unto him;
I will take him to live together
in the holy estate of matrimony.

Seconds later, she hears her own trembling voice mur-
nuring such words as: "better, worse; sickness, health;
·icher, poorer." Before God and a company of witnesses,
vith her beloved, she has made a solemn vow: to live to-
iether, whatever comes!

Truly, the moment is an eloquent one. It speaks the
enderness and strength of true devotion. There is the
1ope of only beautiful days ahead, accented by the truth
hat some clouds could come. There is, above all, the
oyalty of *love*, that can take the bright and dark and blend
hem to a soft, appealing hue; can take, as well, *all bright*
)r *all dark* — the bright, and keep it glowing; the dark, and
nake it rich. Together!

God used the strongest word He could find to express the idea that a husband and wife should live together (Gen. 2:24). "Cleave," God's word, is to be joined fast together, to be glued, cemented. *A husband and wife are to live together.*

If the loyalty of love can be heard clearly in the young bride's sweet, soft-spoken "I will," it sings out even clearer in the life of every woman who keeps her sacred promise and sacred place — by his side, whatever comes! Women such as: Mrs. A, and her daughter, Mrs. B; Mr. Bigg's companion, and Mr. Little's wife; Mr. Aquila's partner, and Mr. Smith's nurse; all women who have learned what it means to be *by his side.*

BY HIS SIDE, WHEREVER HE GOES. Mrs. A might be described as "the girl who had everything!" Beauty, intelligence, a wealthy husband, and a fine home. Imagine how she must have felt when, one day, out of a clear blue sky, her husband announced, "Pack all our things, dear. We're leaving this place."

"A trip? For how long? Where to?" These would be logical questions, but the answers to them would make little sense to most wives.

"Not a *trip* — for *good. I don't know where. God* knows." True to her sacred promise, Mrs. A went with her husband, cheerfully, from place to place, making a home for him in each place he chose to settle. Their journey covered hundreds of perilous miles, and a good many adventurous years. She was an old woman when the A's finally settled down, but her outlook remained youthful and encouraging.

When, quite late in life, her only child was born, Mrs.

A's joy overflowed. "I have given him a son!" Always her first concern was for her husband's happiness. She stayed in her favorite place, by his side, for well over a hundred years. When she died, her husband spent a small fortune on an appropriate burial site for his beloved.

Because Mrs. A, with her outward advantages, remained inwardly modest, unspoiled, flexible, hospitable, unselfish, and obedient, Mr. A could serve his God and his fellow man acceptably. Through her faith in God, and her obedience to her husband, *both Sarah and Abraham were able to be used by God in a most marvelous way* (Read Genesis 12-23):

> ... and in thee shall all the families of the earth be blessed. — Genesis 12:3
>
> ... and in thy seed shall all the nations of the earth be blessed; because thou hast obeyed my voice. — Genesis 22:18
>
> ... to Abraham and his seed were the promises made ... And to thy seed which is Christ. — Galatians 3:16.

The son of Abraham, through whom the promised Christ should come, was Isaac, Sarah's most outstanding contribution.

Not every wife can give birth to a child of such importance to all generations. But every wife can be a "Mrs. A" in honoring her marriage vow, which means *by his side, wherever he goes.*

Sarah has many daughters. The Lord said, ". . . . Sarah obeyed her husband, calling him Lord . . . whose daughters ye are as long as ye do well . . . ." (I Pet. 3:6).

By His Side, When We're Far Apart. One of Sarah's daughters, Mrs. B, the wife of an evangelist, sent her husband a greeting card while he was away on one of his frequent meetings. The message read, "I didn't know I could like anyone so *much* and see so *little* of him!"

Mrs. B. would disagree with those who say, glibly, "Absence makes the heart grow fonder." She knows, better than anyone else, that separate vacations are not the answer to those who *need fonder hearts.* For God, who possesses all wisdom, meant that *living together* would increase, not diminish, a couple's fondness for each other. How easy it would be for one whose husband is regularly away from home for extended periods, to become so caught up in her own pursuits, so concerned with her own self, so independent, *so set in her ways,* that he might become only a familiar visitor in his own home.

Mrs. B's attitude through her husband's absences has never allowed that to happen. "I keep busy," she says, "but not *too* busy." Not too busy sewing and cooking and cleaning the house, to think of him and look forward to having him home; not too busy teaching the children, to remember to write him a letter; not too busy visiting the sick, to find time to pray for his meeting; not too busy praying, to send him a card saying so!

> Above all things have intense and unfailing love for one another . . . — I Peter 4:8, *The Amplified N. T.*

> And let us consider one another to provoke unto love and good works . . . — Hebrews 10:24

The B's togetherness *apart* is possible only because of their togetherness *together.* For "love never fails" (I Cor.

13:18). This is true, not only of evangelists' wives, but of all other "Mrs. B's" who treasure togetherness and make of each separate precious moment together, "a moment to remember." "Nourish" and "cherish" are verbs the Lord used to tell of the thoughtful care and loving esteem of each partner for the other in the closeness of marriage (Eph. 5:29).

Every generation has had its men-on-the-move: soldiers, sailors, salesmen, spacemen. For all such travel-weary husbands, Robert Browning expresses the eagerness to reach home, when love lives there:

> The grey sea and the long black land,
> And the yellow half-moon large and low;
> And the startled little waves that leap
> In fiery ringlets from their sleep,
> As I gain the cove with pushing prow,
> And quench its speed in the slushy sand.
> Then a mile of warm sea-scented beach;
> Three fields to cross till a farm appears;
> A tap at the pane, the quick sharp scratch
> And blue spirt of a lighted match,
> And a voice less loud, thro' its joys and fears,
> Than the two hearts beating each to each!

BY HIS SIDE, ON TOP OF THE HEAP. Some say, "There's room at the top," but many deserving men will never know, because of wives whose personalities, or dispositions, or ineptitudes hold them down. In the business world, this is the day of the husband-wife interview. To be promoted to "Executive's Wife," one must have passed as rigid a test as her husband, in some respects. That our society recognizes the influence of a wife on her husband could not be more clearly demonstrated. Fortunes are involved. And empires are not built by men with un-cooperative wives.

Not all men are attracted by executives' suites, and not all *top* men are *on top*. But when a poor widow who has been used to little finds herself suddenly married to Mr. Bigg, she has placed herself in an unenviable position, in the eyes of most uncovetous women.

The same gentle, lady-like qualities which first attracted a man of his position to this hard-working female field-hand, enabled her to conduct herself always in a manner befitting the wife of such a wealthy and respected gentleman. An entire book in the Bible tells her love story, and wears her lovely name. *Ruth's kindness, her industry, her virtue, and her faith in God are praised by her husband, Boaz, and published in God's Word.*

Ruth's loyalty and undying devotion to her mother-in-law is an "old, old story" which continues to impress and inspire, even in this sometimes disrespectful age. No doubt, Ruth's loyalty to Naomi first attracted Boaz to her side. She never lost it.

Some women cannot survive the temptations which new wealth often brings. Some marriages are wrecked on the "rocks" which money has bought. But Ruth was of a thankful nature. At Boaz's first favor, she had fallen on her face and bowed herself to the ground, saying, "Why have I found grace in thine eyes, that thou shouldst take knowledge of me, seeing I am a stranger?" (2:10). She would not forget to be grateful for her honored place by his side.

The three temptations of being on top are the same ones that plague all people, at every level: lust of the flesh, lust of the eye, and pride of life. But, when a person can buy anything he desires to have, pay for anything he desires to do, and purchase any position he desires to be, life loses its soothing simplicity, to say the least. Often God is choked out by the *cares* that come with wealth. The air can be thin, above the clouds. In the dizzying atmosphere, many have lost their heads.

But not all. Faith in Christ can keep a couple from losing their perspective, through poverty or prosperity. And a wife's attitude toward her husband's worldly success often determines his own reactions.

"In every new city we entered, it was always my wife who made sure, *on Saturday night*, that we would find a place to meet with Christians for worship on Sunday morning," said a man on top of the world, in professional golf. How could he have forgotten old friends, forsaken old ideals, failed to give thanks, with such a wife by his side?

To have a godly companion is to have great wealth, whether rich or poor. But to a man who has achieved what the world calls *Success*, a humble, God-fearing wife is also his surest protection. "For what is a man profited, if he shall gain the whole world, and lose his own soul? . . ." (Matt. 16:26).

By His Side When the Bottom Falls Out. "One day in 1942," a West Texas teacher wrote in her memoirs, "I came home from high school and asked my father, 'When was this *depression* everybody's always talking about?'

"Daddy's blue eyes twinkled. With a wink meant for Mother, he said, 'You children didn't know we were having hard times, but your mother sure did!'

"Then, he laughed more loudly than I had ever heard him laugh, when Mother asked, quite seriously, 'I did? Well — *when was it, Daddy?*' "

The teacher's parents had not lost a fortune overnight, for they had never had one to lose. But, like so many other families during the Great Depression, they had been reduced, rather suddenly, from plenty to what amounted to want. Yet, because her parents had taken the blow so courageously, and so quietly, their children never once guessed that *they* were "the poor and needy" which their Sunday School teacher talked about.

Some families, like the Littles, have lost great wealth in sudden and unexpected ways. "When, in disgrace with fortune and men's eyes," as Shakespeare wrote, many men have lost their reason. Not Mr. Little. To have jumped off a building would never have entered his mind. For it would have put an end to all the renewed excitement he felt in living!

"We are young again!" Mrs. Little explains. "We find ourselves sharing, once again, the joy that comes from simple things. The thrill of accomplishment can be a much bigger one when one's means are small. Do you know, I can prepare nearly fifty-seven different varieties of *hamburger*?"

Unlike Job's wife, and her counterparts, Mrs. Little has not let misfortune misplace the magic words, "We have each other. And we have God!" (See I Tim. 6:6-8). Because of his wife's attitude, Mr. Little can cheerfully refer to himself as having *advanced backwards,* adding, with a smile, "Sooner or later, I suppose, I shall be forced to *flee forward!*"

By His Side, Day in and Day out. Priscilla, the wife of Aquila, is the New Testament's model for all women who are business partners with their husbands. Their business certainly would have flourished today, with the upsurge of interest in the "Great Outdoors," for they were tent-makers. They would have been equivalent to today's construction workers, since, in the First Century, many a man's home was his tent.

Their work was hard, the hours long; and, from their frequent re-locations it would seem that their work was also seasonal and unsteady. Priscilla's understanding must have helped her husband to adjust to each new "territory," just as her energy and skill assisted him in marketing his product, and her pleasant, outgoing personality aided him in maintaining good customer relations.

The same admirable character traits made Priscilla one of the Bible's successful women in two other fields, which to many women would be even harder than building tents! She was a successful *hostess*, and a successful *teacher!*

She extended Christian hospitality to all. The apostle Paul lived in her home in Corinth; in Ephesus, her home was the meeting place for the church. Apollos understood "the way of the Lord more perfectly" because of Priscilla's teaching ability (Read Acts 18:1-3; 19-21; 24-28; Rom. 16:3,4; II Tim. 4:19).

If Aquila's wife and business partner could find the time and the strength to practice true hospitality and obey the Great Commission, today's "Junior Partner" cannot use, "I work with my husband," as an excuse for neglect. Modern Priscillas are *valuable* women, working with their hands, their heads, and their hearts. Working quietly, but constantly, and successfully.

What more richly satisfying life could any woman want than this? To be by her husband's side, shoulder to shoulder, day in and day out — living, loving, working, teaching, entertaining, and praying, *together!*

BY HIS BEDSIDE. Mr. Smith's "nurse" is Mrs. Job's antithesis. They have but one thing in common: sick husbands. Instead of moaning, "Curse God and die!" (Job 2:9), when Mrs. Smith, a frail little grandmother, first learned that her husband's illness would be a chronic and incurable one, she prayed:

"Dear Father, let me learn the right things to do for my darling, and let me develop the strength to do them!"

For over five years, now, Mrs. Smith has spent many hours every day by her husband's bedside, cheering him, comforting him, encouraging him. She has spent most hours every night studying, planning, preparing, and *praying* for the next day. The now so precious day!

Though Mr. Smith remains bedfast, and his body is gradually dying, his spirit remains healthy and vigorous. Physicians who examine him leave his room, shaking their heads. "Remarkable!" one exclaimed. "By all known laws, he should have been dead two years ago!" He probably would have been, without the good medicine of the good nurse by his side (See Prov. 17:22).

Love like Mrs. Smith's does not need to repeat the words, "in sickness and in health." That promise, made so long ago, has for so long gone without saying. Were it not for her husband's frequent pain and forced confinement, she would not hesitate to count these the richest years of her life (Read I Cor. 13).

"God blest me with a good husband," she explains. "He always took good care of me and the children. And now, God is allowing me to take good care of him."

The *loyalty* of love. It can be heard in the words of Mrs. Smith. It can be seen in the life of every faithful wife for whom "by his side" has come to mean *by his bedside,* "to love and to cherish, in sickness . . ."

The loyalty of love, first *heard* in a young bride's "I will," takes on form and substance, to *appear* in all its radiant, full-grown beauty, in the lives of faithful women who *stay close by their husbands' sides, whatever comes.*

XII

Through the Years

A T Helen's wedding, her best friend sang a popular song of the day. It spoke of smiling through the years.

Last June, Helen's oldest daughter was graduated from college and married, all in the same week. Helen's youngest, who is engaged to be married, sang "Through the Years," while Helen sat beside their father, *smiling* through her tears.

The girls can remember very few times in their lives when their mother was not wearing a smile. Having been the fortunate children of their parents' happy marriage, each girl has nothing but high hopes and great expectations for her own.

Helen, too, has high hopes for the years ahead. She remembers her own parents, who made each succeeding year "better than the last!" by their continuing delight in being allowed to live those years together. Having smiled through the early years, and most of the middle years, Helen expects to go on smiling through the years that are left. She believes, "the best is yet to be."

This does not mean that there are no problems to solve, no hurdles to jump, no obstacles to overcome in a truly happy marriage. Helen, her parents, and her daughter have all had some trials and some disappointments, as all other husbands and wives have had, and shall have. But, such experiences always seem to make a good marriage better. As, through love and courage, the storms are weathered, the two who have survived them emerge even closer and more courageous than they were before.

This is that "most marvelous thing" of which Sir Hugh Walpole wrote:

> The most wonderful of all things, I believe, is the discovery of another human being with whom one's relationship has a glowing depth, beauty, and joy as the years increase. This inner progressiveness of love between two human beings is a most marvelous thing. . . .
>
> From *WHAT IS HAPPINESS*. By permission of Putnam's & Coward-McCann.

There are some words of practical advice and warning from those who have experienced the inner progressiveness of love to those who are just beginning. *Each period, through the years, has its own watch words*:

Through the first years, the watchword is *yourself*. Watch yourself. It isn't the easiest thing on earth to switch from "I" feelings to "we" attitudes.

Helen's daughter, but newly married, knows already that it is all too easy in the beginning to think only of one's own pleasure: "Am I *getting* all I expected out of marriage?" instead of "Am I *giving* my best to this marriage?"

In every separate room of the new home, the word *yourself* is worth watching! For, to seek not one's own happiness, but the happiness of another, is a rule which must be applied to every phase of the marriage relationship. Only after careful, dedicated practice can the new bride learn what it seems she should have known all along —

the one who brings joy into the life of another will surely have it for herself (Read I Cor. 13; Acts 20:35).

Watch yourself, when you feel like crying because he won't even eat *one* of your cranberry-carrot juice muffins.

Watch yourself, when you're tempted to go back to sleep and let him *scramble his own eggs,* for a change.

Watch yourself, when you're thinking of keeping on the dirty old duster until *after* he comes home for lunch.

Watch yourself, when you're about to spend more than he makes in a *week* — on *one dress.*

Watch yourself, when *your* work begins to seem like *drudgery,* compared to *his.*

Watch yourself, when you're contemplating ways to *punish* him for *daring* to *disagree* with *you.*

Watch yourself, especially, when you're unwilling to share him with anybody or anything. For to limit another's horizons, is to shrink, also, one's self. Your own selfish over-possessiveness can deny him this right to the accomplishment that would bless both your lives.

Yourself is the watchword for the early years. *Watch it!*

Through the middle years, the watchword is *growing.* All who have survived the changes of middle-age would say, "Watch out for these *growing things:*"

The growing desire for softness and ease. Try to keep your youthful enthusiasm, and your husband will keep his. *Life isn't half over, yet!* (Read Lk. 12:19).

The growing influence of the crowd upon your life. You

don't *have* to conform, in all respects, to those around you. Add interest to their lives, and zest to your own, by daring to be different — *when the difference makes sense* (Read Rom. 12:2).

The growing love of money. Remember, *money worship is a root,* from which no good, only *evil,* can spring. If you doubt it — look around you! (Read I Tim. 6:10).

The growing passion to indulge your appetite. Middle-aged doesn't *have* to mean *fat!* (Read. Gal. 5:23; II Pet. 1:6).

The growing tendency to take your husband for granted. If there were *ever* to be an *appropriate time,* this would not be it. Remember, *he's* going through *those dangerous middle years,* himself (Read Heb. 10:24; Titus 2:4).

The growing temptation to stop growing. Keep active in mind, as well as in soul. You haven't yet *learned* it *all,* and you haven't yet *attained perfection* — as your husband would probably tell you, if he dared! (Read II Pet. 1:5; 3:18).

Watch yourself through the early years, watch your growing through the middle years, and *through the older years, watch your rejections.*

Helen's mother and father left her a priceless heritage. They discovered the Fountain of Youth: the realization that the only way to remain young is to grow old gracefully. Instead of nursing the notion that they are *being rejected,* aging couples must check their own impulses to reject the very things that can make the older years the *best* years.

All who have experienced the richness of those years would echo, "Watch":

Rejection of age. The Lord demonstrated his respect for age when he instructed that congregations should be led by the elder men, and that the elder women should teach the younger women. *Respect your own age — it is an accomplishment, in God's eyes* (Read Acts 14:23; Titus 1:5; 2:4).

Rejection of responsibilities. There are challenging responsibilities connected with the older years. Your children may be grown up and gone, but now you have *time* for *other* children, *freedom* to *do* for other children. Men will have acquired the wisdom, judgment, and necessary character to be teachers of boys, lifters of society and good elders in the church; women, the knowledge and skill to be "teachers of good things" to the younger women (Titus 1:6-9; 2:2-5). *Accept your responsibilities, and you will be too busy to feel rejected.*

Rejection of "retirement." It's only a word. *Look upon it as a change of work, not an end to work.* Retirement is a fresh, new beginning. It is a time for new interests, new attention to old interests, new knowledge, new places, new faces. Above all, it is a time, at long last, *for each other.* (Read Philippians 4:11; Heb. 13:5; I Tim. 6:6-8).

Rejection of the children's leaving. The Lord knew best — ". . . a man shall leave father and mother . . ." (Gen. 2:23,24). Let them go. Your married children must have sufficient liberty to grow, to make their own mistakes and learn by them, just as you did. You, also, must have freedom to try your own new wings, without too much well-meant advice from those whom you taught to fly!

As grandparents, have the courage to say to your children, "Let us be!"

> Be around, but never hovering.
> Be interested, but never anxious.
> Be helpful, but never interfering.
> Be independent, but never ungracious.
> Be available as a baby-sitter, but never
> soliciting business!
> Be, above all, an example:
> . . . faithful unto death. — Rev. 2:10

Rejection of the idea of death. A child of God accepts death as a necessary part of life. Surrender to God the loved ones who have died. Many times the older years are made miserable by the morbid and useless mourning for those who have gone to be with the Lord. Recognize this type of rejection for what it is: not undying loyalty to one's dead, but unbecoming pity for one's self. Recognize, also, what it actually accomplishes: it dishonors the dead; it disgusts the living; it denies the faith.

Instead of wallowing in your grief, rejoice in your memories that neither time nor death can steal. Rejoice in the knowledge that the loved one has reached the blessed state which the inspired apostle said "is far far better" (Philippians 1:23). Rejoice that you can go on living for the living (Job 10:12; Philippians 1:21). Rejoice that God can heal your broken heart, and use the strength you gain through sorrow, to His glory (Psalms 147:3; Philippians 1:29). Rejoice, and ". . . sorrow not even as others which have no hope" (I Thess. 4:13).

Rejection of mental activity. Contrary to popular opinion, the mind never grows old. The brain may age, and often there is some physical impairment that impedes the thinking. But, more often, what is called a "senile mind" is a mind that lags because of a lack of mental exercise. *Older couples have time to read*: read good books to each other, discuss what you read. Read the newspapers. Discuss the news, express *your* views, and listen to *his*.

Read the Word of God faithfully — morning, noon and night. Examine each passage as carefully and as curiously as you would read a brand-new best-selling book! You will never cease to find in the Old Book *new lessons* to challenge and inspire. Whatever your particular need might be, "All scripture . . . is profitable . . ." (II Tim. 3:16). If you will fill your mind with the Word of God, it will never be empty, and *you will never be too old to think*.

Through the years, *smiling*. It is a precious promise, and a *worthy aim*. It is *entirely possible*, also, with one's hand in God's hand, one eye watching for danger signals along the way, and the other eye looking forward, eagerly, to the wonderful years ahead.

Henry Van Dyke has spoken for all who enter into marriage with high hopes and great expectations:

> Let me but live my life from year to year
> With forward face and unreluctant soul.
> Not hastening to, nor turning from the goal;
> Not mourning for the things that disappear
> In the dim past, nor holding back in fear
> From what the future veils; but with a whole
> And happy heart, that pays its toll
> To youth and age, and travels on with cheer.
> . . . . I shall grow old, but never lose life's zest,
> Because the road's last turn will be the best.

From <i>"THE THREE BEST THINGS."</i>
By permission of Charles Scribner's Sons, publishers.

XIII

Till Death Us Do Part

They talk and talk
  of life and death, and death and life,
  and whether, when we've gone
  from life to death, to life again,
  we'll know each other still.
They talk, and turn to passages
  that prove we won't; (Lk. 20:34,35; I Cor. 15:44-50)
They talk, and point out places
  where it shows we will; (Jno. 21:2; ICor. 15:20; Jno. 3:5)
They talk and turn, and talk and prove,
And talk and point, and talk and show,
And talk, and talk, and talk!

  AND I BELIEVE THEM ALL. (Jno. 17:17)

But I believe this, too:
  that God loves you,
  and God loves me,
  and God knows we've loved each other!
Why talk at all?

Perhaps the poet talked too much
  or had too much of talk:
  "O thou soul of my soul! I shall clasp
    thee again,
  And with God be the rest!"

But THOU, soul of MY soul,
  believe with me:
    since God has ever loved us both,
    and given us to love each other here,
    His perfect love, continuing,
    WE NEED NOT FEAR. (I Cor. 13:13; I Jno. 4:16-18)

Let them talk.

"I shall clasp thee again,
And with God be the REST!"
    is all we need to say,
    except, in faith, to add:
    "With God, also, be the FIRST!" (Lk. 11:2).

— Lois Terry